LIFEQUAKES

Cover design, illustration, photography and all contents of
this book are © Deborah DeLisi (www.delisiart.com)

ISBN-13: 978-1515011453
ISBN-10: 1515011453

Printed by CreateSpace, An Amazon.com Company
First printing March 2016

Available from DeLisiArt.com, Amazon.com,
CreateSpace.com, and other retail outlets

LIFEQUAKES
The Journey Through Loss and Grief

Words, Illustrations & Photographs by
Deborah DeLisi

DEDICATED
To My Daughters
Sara and Kate,
One on Earth
One in Heaven

ACKNOWLEDGMENTS

So many have helped me move through my grief after the loss of my youngest daughter. Firstly, I acknowledge my daughter Sara, for moving through an impossible event by my side, and for her partner Jared, for holding her up best of all.

To Bill, whose loss is equal to mine, and to those who helped me through the first month and beyond: Joe, Diane & Bob, Lynne, David, Paul, Stacey, Mary, Pepper, Chris and Lois. For you, I am forever grateful.

To the California Crew who saved my hide: Mary and Todd, Janis and Doug, Kat, Bea and more. You held me together.

Abundant thanks to my friends that reached out to me from faraway places: Eva, Simone, Liew, Bec, Nell, Cynthya, Libby, Anders & Cacina, Lee, and all those who took the time to call and email. It helped more than you know.

With gratitude to my customers who financially supported me immediately after my loss, when I was struggling in every possible way. You know who you are and I will never forget you.

To Kate's friends: Tammie, Erika, Holley & Bryan, Bri, and others in NH, NC and FL: I love all of you.

My beach, the stones, and nature: You saved my sanity on a daily basis.

And to all who know what a Lifequake is, you will make it with help from those around you. Please ask for it and let others in.

If it takes a village to raise a child, it also takes a village to help those who lose one. Thank you to my village.

LIFEQUAKES

Your kids are not supposed to die before you do. Everyone knows that. And especially not by ending their own life. The rules of life seemed to become far more unfair when my 29-year-old daughter, Kate, lost her battle with depression on September 8, 2014. She is gone and, yet, somehow I am still here. I am also somewhere else.

I woke up on the morning of September 9, 2014 wondering where that somewhere else was. The room was unfamiliar: white curtains, cold pillow, and the droning chatter coming from another room. Where was I? My brain answered with a jolting flashback to yesterday: I was at my sister's house in North Carolina. The painful recall of the last 24 hours crushed every dream I ever had. My insides ached as if I was forced to swallow the Titanic and all the imploding torment that accompanies flawed decisions. Crying felt so limiting because my grief wanted to become a scream that projected from deep inside me and raced towards the

stratosphere, becoming the biggest, most colossal tornado the world had ever seen. I didn't want to remember yesterday, but I had to. I didn't want to be alive, but I was. Most of all, I wish I was never born. But I was.

I was born in New York City on a very ordinary day in a very ordinary way. My mom wasn't even awake when I was born. She said the doctors put her in a state of 'twilight sleep' when she was about to deliver. My mother has never been able to tell me who I was named after or why she picked the name Deborah for me. But it was better than being named after my Nonnie, whose name was Enelda. As the second of six kids—three boys and three girls—I was the big sister to Diane and Lynne. Joe was my big brother and he never excluded me from playing ball with him. Dave and Paul were born after Lynne and close in age. As kids they practiced Brotherly Shove more than Brotherly Love. We're all so different, but we all love each other deeply.

In my family I was known as the one who liked to draw all the time. I came into this world with one talent: I am creative. Zooming in on that broad word, I make a living as an artist. We are here to show the world *our world*, through our eyes, and from many perspectives and possibilities. There's a lot of enjoyment to be gained from writing, doodling, playing, inventing and imagining. Ask any creative type. But don't ask me to join a gym, go on a strenuous hike or work in a cubicle. That isn't part of my DNA. Instead, my artist's path seems to have placed me in front of audiences at metaphysical events in the US and Europe. It's been an uplifting and soul-satisfying experience to teach people about the innate creative aspects that lie dormant

in each of us. Babies and children are the most creative beings on the planet. Just try hiding a box of cookies or a favorite toy from a kid, and you'll see the amazingly creative ways that they will find their way to it *and get it.* Ask a room full of 5-year olds *"Who can draw? Who is good at singing?"* They all raise their hands. Ask the same questions to a room full of 20-year olds, and only a few will hesitantly admit to having a morsel of creativity. It's still there but its brilliance gets obscured by wrapping itself in layers of judgment from within and without. I like to help people shed those layers and reignite that ember of creativity inside them. It's magical to witness that.

Often, at the seminars and workshops I attend, people arrive looking for a sense of what's-up-on-planet-earth, and they leave feeling very positive about the direction we humans are headed. Joining together as some type of pop-up community, we fill our collective soul with good vibes and good chat about our individual futures. We feel the ripples of hope and meaning reach our heart and personal life. And it *should* be this way. We need to gather with like-minded people and kindred spirits to affirm that we're not alone in our vision for this world and for ourselves. We all need to believe that this earth experience is inherently a good one, and our actions and reaffirming thoughts are creating positive movement for the planet. This keeps us going.

But what happens when we leave these
uplifting gatherings?
And we're home…
     Going about our daily lives…
          And then…

Something happens.
    A trauma.
        A personal tragedy.

Something that shakes your world and rattles your foundation so profoundly that you drop to your knees crying for it not to be so. What happens when your life is hit by a magnitude 9.0 shock on your own personal Richter scale?

This is a Lifequake.

Sometimes life's experiences come at us with such a force that it does not feel like the "light and love" lantern that we carry to illuminate our next steps. How does a person deal with—and move through—the aftermath of a Lifequake? Let me begin with the events leading up to *my* death on September 8, 2014.

For the last decade I've been collaborating with a luminary research scientist and medical doctor in California who embraces hard science, emerging technology and metaphysics in one seamless career. We work together on an esoteric project called The Pineal Tones. I create the visionary art that accompanies his seminars where participants learn the use of voice and sound-frequency as a tool for balance and broader human potential. This isn't a career path I could have envisioned when majoring in graphic design in Connecticut, but it's taken both of us around the globe teaching popular workshops. Our collaboration has been a remarkable journey of expansion and opening up to many possibilities for all human beings and the planet.

One of the possibilities-turned-reality was that in late 2013

I gave up my home in California and made plans to live a year of bold adventure. I would travel The Dharma Highway, a name a friend suggested for my freedom-inspired trek. The philosophy was to travel where invited to teach workshops—anywhere in the world—and trust that the universe had my back. Off I went to Hawaii, Mt. Shasta, Canberra, Melbourne, Brisbane, Queensland, and Lisbon.

Adventures are great for renewing the soul and giving us a gift that says, "Here, open this box. It's your life. Isn't it beautiful and unique?" Ten months on the Dharma Highway provided many such gifts, and I was looking forward to September workshops in Portugal. I love the people there and was excited to return to teach a workshop in a place so similar to my beloved California. Four days after arriving in sunny and breezy Lisbon, my Lifequake struck, exploding my reality with the force of 20,000 tons of dynamite and blasting me 3,900 miles all the way back to America. The shock is one I do not know how to recover from, and the emotional shrapnel is embedded in my scars forever.

Kate had taken an overdose of acetaminophen while I was helplessly far away. My sister, Diane, contacted me with the news that Kate had called 911 and was taken to a hospital in Charlotte, North Carolina, about 2 hours from Kate's home. My brain was not comprehending the information I was hearing or what was going on, and worse yet, I was alone in a far away country. When I learned that Kate was in the hospital, I never fathomed that this was life threatening. Something as ordinary as acetaminophen pills—my brain told me that maybe she had really bad cramps? Panic didn't set in until I spoke to the nurse that was caring for Kate in the emergency room. In a very direct manner, she let me know it was urgent that I get to Kate's bedside. Then she handed the phone to the doctor who used words like liver failure...liver transplant *if we can get one*...coma... could even *result in death*. But she was alive and breathing, and I needed to get to that hospital and bring along all the ingredients that make a miracle, if only I knew them.

A mother learns to feel a whole panorama of emotions when it comes to caring for their kids, but not this emotion. It's an emotion so fiery that getting near it can cause spontaneous combustion of a life and a quick ticket to the worst kind of living hell.

When I got off the phone with the hospital, my reality felt unlike anything I can put words to. Was it like standing in the gallows with a noose on my neck, knowing that at any second, the floor was going to drop from under me? Yes. Did it feel like I was being disemboweled by sadistic invisible forces? Yes. Were my insides shaking like an airplane falling apart in mid-air? Even more so. What about those mythological people who were thrown into volcanoes while still alive? Was it like that? More than you know. For the next 10 hours my emotions ricocheted around my body like crazy insects. I was helpless. Alone. Terrified and paralyzed, unable to do a damn thing to help my daughter.

Night was not for resting, and the next morning, I boarded a flight from Portugal to New Jersey and then on to North Carolina. What would await me there? I did not know whether Kate's health or my reality was going to zig or zag in the direction I was willing it to go. The surreal way in which realities can collide is disarming and without resolution. The equation was something like this:

Want to Die Today + Want to Live Tomorrow = Death Now x People in Family. It made no sense, I had no control over the situation and the feeling of helplessness was amplified a million fold.

After flying for what seemed like days of suspended animation, I arrived in Newark, New Jersey. Waiting for me was my pal Stacey, my best friend since 1966. We'd been through a lot together, and she was by my side, meeting me in Newark as we headed for Charlotte. Weary and teary, she and I arrived in North Carolina in the late afternoon of September 8. The bizarre routine of baggage claim and airport pickup areas seemed so out of sync this time. Half hour to the hospital I was told, by my brother-in-law behind the wheel. Diane was in the front seat next to her husband, and I tip-toed into a conversation about Kate's condition and failing liver.

"Is she jaundiced?" "Yes."

"On the phone you said her IV made her look a little puffy. Is that still true?" "Yes."

I asked if Sara, my older daughter and Kate's only sister, was there waiting for me. "MmmHmm" Diane slowly replied and nodded yes. And so was my other sister Lynne, and my niece Christina.

I asked if there was anything else I should know before arriving at the hospital. This time Bob responded with a gentle but immediate "Yes." My eyes darted to Diane.

I watched all color drain from her face as she sat motionless. I had seen that happen to her once before. We were little kids at an amusement park where there were fake cowboys having a make-believe gunfight in a corral. All the kids gathered around the split-rail fence as the sheriff and the outlaw argued and made escalating threats at each other. Suddenly, the outlaw grabbed Diane and picked her up, using her as a human shield against the sheriff that was shooting "bullets" at him. I will never forget the look on her face—or my shock—in thinking she was about to die.

I looked at Diane in the front seat, and although her mouth was moving in strange and twisting ways no words were coming out. Insanity was rushing into my headspace as I methodically formed the words "*Is….she….still….alive….?*" Diane silently shook her head side to side, and in that instant my reality shook violently and disconnected me from my life up until that point. In that instant I died. Cause of death: spontaneous combustion of a soul. Place of residence: hell.

Gone. Forever. Forever Not Here. Diane had the impossible task of letting me know Kate had died 90 minutes earlier. As shock took over, I put my hands over my ears and yell-cried over and over, "I can't hear this! I can't hear this! I can't hear this! Don't tell me this! I don't want to hear this!" I was in an odd dimension where you exist alive and dead simultaneously. I was hung in the gallows, disemboweled, shaken apart in a plane wreck and thrown into the volcano with eyes wide open. A Lifequake.

I always told my daughters that of all the artwork I ever made, they were my two best creations. Sara and Kate were my beautiful masterpieces, my legacy. They still are.

Kate was an impractical idealist and she never hesitated to tell you her view of how things should really be. Most of her ideas were funny, some were ridiculous, and others seemed brilliant. She was the radiant-yet-stubborn person that I was proud to call my daughter. Even beyond that, she was my friend. We had a lot of fun together on trips to New York, concerts, shopping, talks on the couch, and gardening. She was my second born, and younger sister to Sara. Most of their lives, my girls remember our family as the three of us. Their dad and I divorced when they were 7 and 4 years old.

Kate and I shared a love of science, nature, physics, music and the mysteries of here and the great beyond. Sara and Kate shared an appreciation for the silly side of life, fun with their step brother Steven, modern cartoon humor, and the things sisters share, which is probably sharing stories about stupid things parents say and do.

Although Kate had struggled with depression and Lyme disease, we noticed that she seemed to be doing quite good, feeling happier and witnessing her life unfolding in a more positive way. She just landed the job she wanted and found a place to live with people she enjoyed getting to know. Three weeks prior to her unforeseen death, Stacey and I visited with her in North Carolina. We shared nine days of fun, laughter, delightful food, chit-chat and sightseeing in the Smokies and Blue Ridge Mountains. She loved those mountains. Kate and I had a great time together during that final visit, and left each others company with big, big hugs. We made tentative plans to visit again over Thanksgiving at Sara's house in Seattle.

I left that visit optimistic for Kate. When family members asked me how she was doing I told them, "She's finally launched!" Stacey and I were her two moms, and we were thrilled to see her doing what she dreamed of and living in the town of her choosing: Asheville.

I'm sharing some of Kate's back story with you because it's important to know that NOTHING can prepare you for a Lifequake. You never see them coming. But they happen.

They are like earthquakes, but remember this: they have no fault lines. No one is at fault when a Lifequake happens, and lacking a fault line, there is no way to predict when or where the quake will occur.

A Lifequake has a magnitude of 7.0 and up. It disassembles your world in a few seconds, disconnects you from the reality you were living in and instantly shoves you in a new one that you really don't want to be in.

You're plunged into grief and loss, left amidst the rubble, in a place that kind of looks like your life…the environment is familiar, the people are recognizable…but it's not the same. Life is completely different now, and maybe those around you don't see that you feel like an alien in your own world. What do you do now? How do you handle being catapulted into this life you never imagined? How do you begin to take steps in a life you didn't agree to? How do you function when you're lost in loss?

I'm going to share some of my personal sketches with you from the journal I started after the loss of my daughter. I lived alone and grieved alone and these sketches were where I placed my feelings. In the United States we tend to avoid deep grieving and we have a lack of cultural traditions for processing grief. Most employers only allow three days of bereavement leave when an employee loses a family member. After three days everyone assumes they can return to work, be productive and pick up where they left off. The grieving process has barely started and is nowhere near complete.

Transitioning into a new life without a loved one is accomplished in very small steps that are never linear. My hope for you is that as you read these pages you will realize that you are not alone. Maybe the pages in your journal will serve as stepping stones for the journey through unfamiliar territory. My first steps led me to a place I called "Limbo Land". It's where the edges of your old life and new life overlap and it feels like there's no journeying forward and you can't turn around and go back.

I never thought I'd create art again. I no longer wanted to create anything—and when I did, it went from colorful ethereal art to black pen on brown paper . That was the most I could handle after the color drained out of my world.

My journal pages are like postcards from a new and unfamiliar life and the recipient is someone I love or despise, or both. Going through Kate's few possessions after her passing, I came across many empty journals which Sara and I put aside to donate. Kate loved to write—but she was a perfectionist—and although she intended to fill the pages with her originality, little was ever put on paper. The journals were piled in a corner of my sister's garage ready to be given away.

 My art went from this...

to this

Because you left me,

I FEEL...

HURT ABANDONED ...LOST LOVE

LIKE A SAD CHILD

DEPRESSED LOST ←SEPARATION→ life is unfair

KILLED "NOT QUITE HERE" "LIKE AN OBSERVER"

LOSS OF PURPOSE TRAUMATIZED Deep

Grief SEPARATED

CONFUSION? BROKEN PROMISES

EMPTY SHOCK Heartbroken BETRAYAL DESTROYED

SAD Broken Family WHY? NO WORDS FOR THIS

DESTROYED + DISTRAUGHT you changed my life without my permission CHEATED MAD

PERMANENT LOSS DETACHED LIED TO

DISAPPOINTED

Day Number 125

i am lost in a New Land

and my compass no longer works. Send Help...

That night as I lay in bed in North Carolina, crying, I had the urge to say things to people, yet I didn't really want to talk to anyone. So the next morning I went to the garage, got one of Kate's empty journals and her pens, and started to write what was inside me. It was rarely good, often bad and sometimes ugly. Black pen on brown paper, the thoughts and feelings were released onto paper.

The abrupt changes that a Lifequake delivers are shocking. It's a feeling of life handing you the exact opposite of what you saw for yourself. It's a feeling that the rules life gave you to play by are different than the rules it gives to others. It feels unfair, in a way that makes me want to run up to strangers and scream in their face: "Stop everything you're doing! You could lose everything you love in two seconds!"

I'm letting you know that when a Lifequake hits, *you're*

not alone. Its victims are scattered everywhere, and there is no prejudice for where you live or how much you're worth. These types of traumatic events hit people from every walk of life. Its victims walk among us, carrying the invisible scars of what they've been through, and no one notices.

If you've been through a Lifequake, you've suffered a huge loss—or losses. Perhaps it was the loss of a spouse, a family member, someone you love. Perhaps someone in the military. Maybe you've lost a relationship with something or someone recently: a friend, a job, a home. One can lose stability, a business, financial security, a reputation, or a belief. Kate lost her way in the world, and this inner loss must be deeply acknowledged. When we experience loss, we lose our way too. Your Lifequake may have occurred in childhood, and you didn't have the tools to rebuild from the mess—and you're still walking through it.

Life's cataclysms can rearrange the landscape of your world in the form of illness, a violent crime, an accident, or a betrayal by someone you thought could never do such a thing, but they did.

And then, when you survey the damage and what is left you notice you've also lost most of yourself. Your identity has been blasted to pieces and you feel like you went from being a strong mountain to a pile of gravel. Looking out over this landscape, you find yourself at the precipice of a canyon, deciding what to do, not knowing which way to go and where that next step will take you.

In the days that followed my loss of Kate, I walked around in shock, perhaps even for months. It's hard to tell where

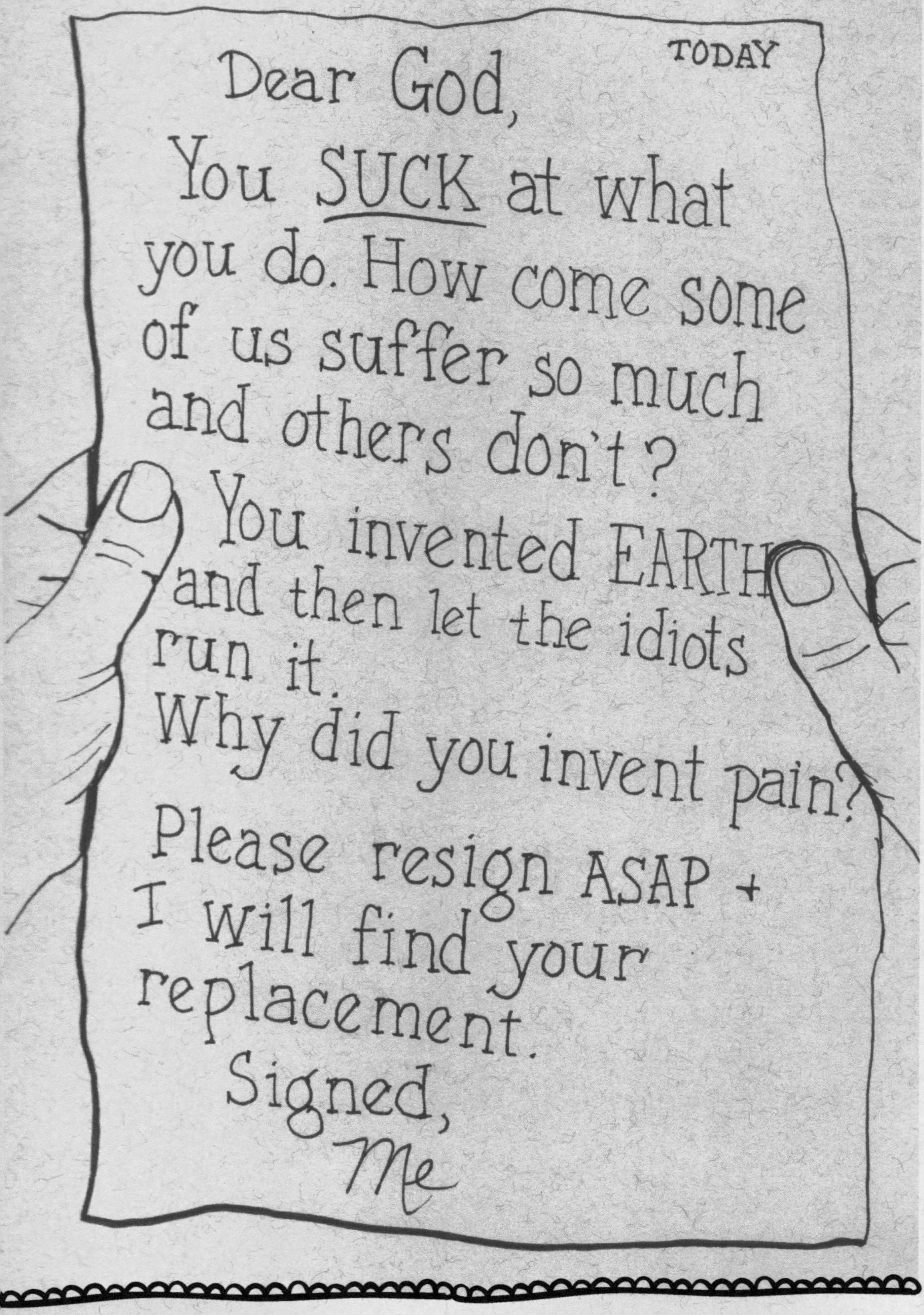
TODAY
Dear God,
You SUCK at what you do. How come some of us suffer so much and others don't?
You invented EARTH and then let the idiots run it.
Why did you invent pain?
Please resign ASAP + I will find your replacement.
Signed,
Me

shock ends and where the permanently altered reality begins. To the outside world, I looked like Regular Deb, but inwardly my psyche was knocked out with a one-two punch directly from the hand of God. I very much wanted to punch him or her back, only twice as hard as I was hit.

What's important here is to acknowledge that life *does* come with *all* the experiences, and pain is one of them. It touches us emotionally, mentally, physically, spiritually or all of the above. The truth is, pain is one of the outcomes we may get when we participate with life.

The truth is: we never stop learning, and life is hard. The truth is: no one leaves this life unscathed in some way.

No one. Not even people we look up to, like spiritual masters or religious figures such as Jesus. Look what experiences life brought him! His life—and the life of any saint—is proof that our time on earth comes with enormous challenges, and the suffering we may experience and endure can be epic.

When you have a Lifequake it extinguishes anything resembling light and pushes you out the door of your comfort zone and into the "Dark Night of the Soul". Here begins a hellish journey through tears, grief and painful contortions that tumble us through a starless universe. All sustaining light has been removed, and you are faced with navigating in the void. Your other senses open up in new ways that replace your eyes. With considerable time—and practice— the darkness becomes slightly less scary to move through. The cycle of the earth around the sun feels less terrifying. I know from experience that as you go through this process

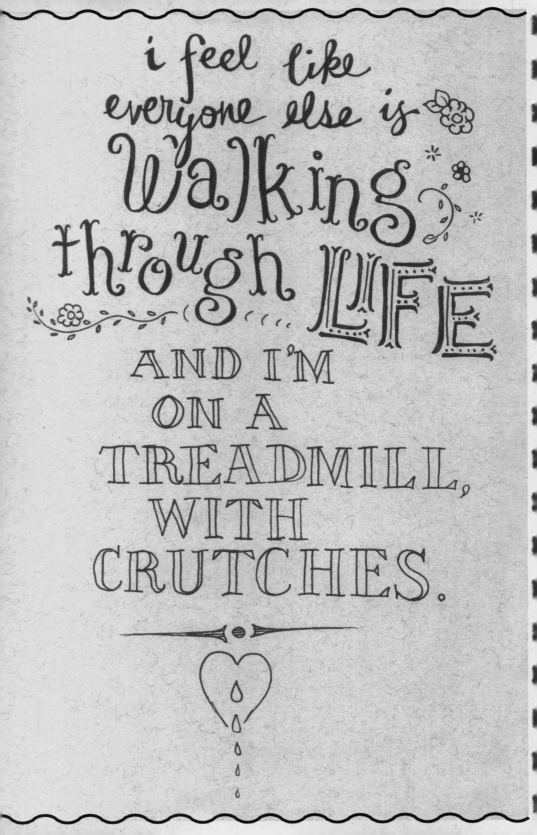

it usually means dividing yourself between a functioning public person and a grieving private one.

When in public, you will notice you've become a really good actor. You can look normal, sound normal, and even tell jokes and laugh in the right places. You remember the right expressions and the right faces to make for people. But when you are alone it is different. The acting gets put aside, and you are faced with the concept of *forever* in this new life, and forever is overwhelming. There is no undoing anything.

The journey through grief and life's hardest moments can be likened to falling into a black wormhole, nature's own way of grieving the death of a star, suppressing all light with its immense gravitational pull. Grief can be like that gravitational pull that light cannot escape, making it appear black to those who observe.

Now, theoretically, if you were to jump onto your trusty dragon and ride it into the black wormhole, physics postulates that you could be sucked down a tunnel (called the Einstein-Rosen bridge) and shot out of a white hole into

a parallel universe. The grief that comes with a Lifequake takes you on that ride.

You can't escape grief, and you can't fix it either. Our species loves to fix things, especially everything that is uncomfortable and unpleasant. But sometimes life hands us broken dreams that cannot be fixed, and as unpleasant as it is, one must move through the tunnel of grief, falling into the darkness, not being able to grab a steady hold of the light, swirling and experiencing this intense pull. Ride through this fierce tunnel, however many light years it takes, until you find you've popped out the other side of the wormhole, into a new landscape, a new reality.

It's not the same place where you entered the tunnel. You're still you, but you're in a new place. Dizzy from the experience, and wondering how you got there, while dusting yourself off from a journey that was not part of Plan A or Plan B. Having a Lifequake was not on your bucket list.

Once you experience a shakeup of this magnitude, you look at everyone you meet and wonder how loss and grief have touched them. Your eyes see the world differently now, and I guess that's the real start of compassion. There's a well-known quote that reads:

"There isn't anyone you couldn't love once you've heard their story."

Mary Lou Kownacki, author

In hearing their story, you'll learn that you have much in common with them, you're not so alone after all. So many share this bond of experiencing a Lifequake that asks us to make friends with the darkness: the parts of life we don't want to face, especially not alone. It's scary, and it frightens us. We long to only experience the happier things in life but in the big picture, there is always balance.

We love it when birds sing their songs and chirp at sunrise on a beautiful day, yet we also admire the song of the crickets at night, and the mysterious owl who fills the night with its echoing call, in the void of sunlight. We look at this creature—the owl—and assign it mystical qualities associated with going within ourselves to find hidden aspects, wisdom being one of them. Like the owl, a Lifequake removes us from the noise of everyday life and asks us to become the silent observer. As we develop the ability to see in the dark, we become adept at piercing through shadows with our intuitive insights. The symbolic owl of the night mirrors inner wisdom that is gained by going through your the dark times. We witness that which is inside of us, the indestructible aspect—or soul—that has the ability to carry us through darkness.

Peering into the places within that seemed too scary to explore, you search for answers to the hard questions. The biggest question being "WHY?" We lack a clear answer. Or any answer. Or maybe it's not the answer we wanted.

In your search to interpret the "why's," the quest moves inward. Like an in-breath traveling to the caverns within, and you look to see what is there. You become a miner of your interior landscape, peering into dark hollows, looking to see what might be discovered. As part of your intimate exploration you may look for light from a divine source to reveal the "why" of your purpose and story.

And then, when you are ready...you exhale...taking your inner understandings into the outside world. It sounds more like an out-breath "ahhhhh" than an "ah ha," and here is the first movement that is given to your grief. It follows the same rhythm as the breath, inward then out-ward. Inner searching gives birth to an understanding that becomes a doorway through which you step into the out-side world. Your odyssey through night will lead towards a horizon that awakens a dusky hint of the first light.

When a Lifequake strikes, the physical tremors ripple into your outside world with the feeling that "this hurts like hell." And inwardly, you quietly acknowledge that your life has changed and the landscape will never look the same. Yet you're still alive, and there's no map or instruction manual on what to do or where to go next. You feel completely lost.

You bargain with your Creator (I yelled at him/her often and loud) and enjoy it! In time—a long time—often years after a trauma, something begins to happen.

The cocoon of grief and confusion that you've been living in, and punching the walls of, slowly starts to loosen up... expand...give way. When you loosen your grip around the trauma you've experienced, you give it permission to change, because *you've* changed, and it no longer can con-tain you. You start to free yourself.

You slowly begin to transform within, like the metaphorical butterfly. You will emerge in your own perfect timing, a different version of yourself. And I stress the word DIFFERENT. Not better, not worse, just different. The caterpillar sees the world from a point of view that's within a certain number of feet off the ground. A butterfly has a greater freedom of movement and can see the world from a perspective that's 20 times higher than the caterpillar. It has transformed and will live the rest of its life seeing from that perspective. As will you.

No matter how hard it tries, a butterfly can never go back to being a caterpillar. And you can never go back to seeing the world the way that you used to. The artist Pablo Picasso said, "There is only one way to see things, until someone shows us how to look at them with different eyes."

Once you have this shift in perspectives, in how you view your world, you may begin to take baby steps into imagining a future that was not possible up until this point. There are many practical and creative ways for tragedy to become a catalyst in one's life, and there is no rush or demand to get to this point. Some may never get there, and that's perfectly okay. For some, having to create a new future is so daunting that a comfort zone is created in "Limbo Land" and they feel safest there, often lingering for their remaining years.

In the initial weeks and months following Kate's passing, I was not ready to hear anything from anyone about how to turn my tragedy into a "gift" or to "find the blessing" in what happened. In fact, I still despise a point of view that says there is a "gift" in losing my daughter because I would trade in all of this and more to have my old life back and Kate still alive.

People try to say the right things to a grieving person and most of it will be taken the wrong way. I became hyper-sensitive to anything anyone said to me, and found reasons to take everything the wrong way. Somehow it seemed right to make everyone wrong, but it didn't make me feel any better. It took time for me to accept that my friends and family were trying to reach me with kindness to me, no matter what words they carefully chose. Softening my pettiness brought me closer to leaving "Limbo Land."

There is no timeline for moving through grief, and I emphasize that you travel at your own pace and allow ALL feelings to be present. In allowing this for myself, it brought about an unexpected change that I couldn't have planned for. I'd like to share this part of my experience and personal story with you.

After my global-living adventure ended abruptly on September 8, 2014, I made my way back to the southern California beach town where I was living before. For a few months, my home was a friends' couch and, as nice as they were to me, I hated what my life had become. Sara lived 1,100 miles away, my siblings were 2,800 miles away, I had no Kate, no home, and after my workshops were canceled in Europe, no income. I felt robbed of everything.

I was hanging on by a thread, barely. I spent many mornings walking the beach alone. Mornings are cloudy on the coast, but sunglasses were mandatory for hiding my tear-streaked face. I walked with my head down, crying, looking at the sand and the water at my feet. I would talk to the ocean as if it were Kate. Each step I took was a baby step moving me out into the world again, even if I didn't want to be there. These were clumsy and painful baby steps and not always in a forward direction. Looking at the other early morning beach walkers and joggers, I noticed that taking their steps seemed easier than mine. With long strides and enthusiasm they jogged right past me. I was invisible. I was crippled by my loss, and no one noticed. Our society isn't comfortable with very sad people or invading someone's privacy by offering a hug to a stranger.

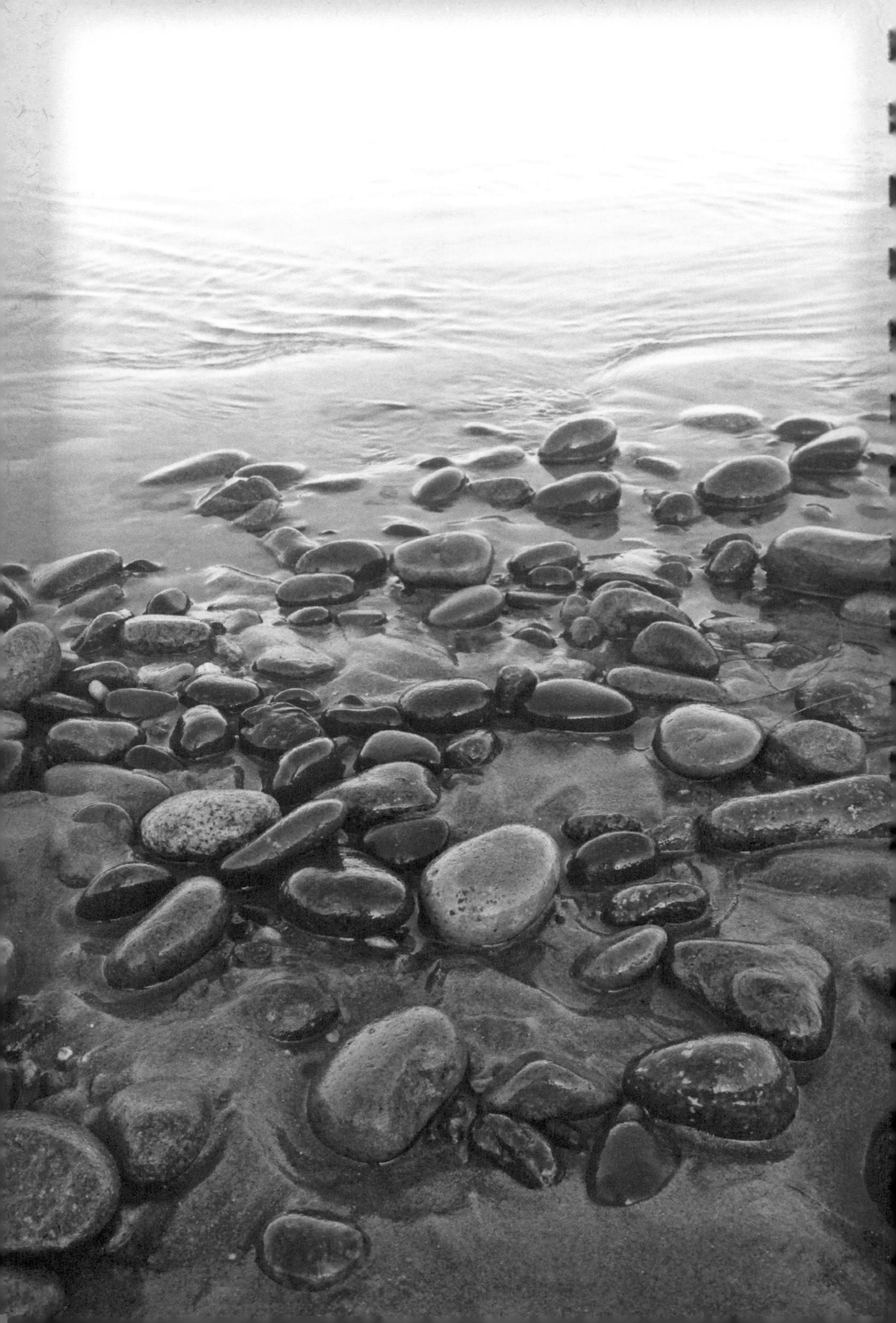

I could have used one. With all the times I cried in restaurants, grocery stores, retail stores, on airplanes and beach walks, not one person made eye contact with me. Grievers are a see-through segment of the population, making it more painful.

After a few months of solitary beach walks, I began to notice that there were a large number of stones on my beach. (I liked to call it *my beach* since I was often the only one there on early winter mornings.) I also liked that the stones on my beach seemed to ask nothing of me. Inanimate objects with blank stares. Good, that's how I liked it. They didn't ask me the horrible question: "How are you?" And I didn't have to interact with them. I could even throw them long and far if I wanted to. And because they asked nothing of me, I allowed them to become friends that I would visit each morning.

And because I didn't have to have to chat with the stones, I could get to know them by observing them. I noticed their shapes: ovalish. Texture: smooth. They looked like miniature extinct planets from an underwater galaxy. My rocky pals began to captivate me, and I started bringing one or two home.

The stones and I had a lot in common. Like the owls, we were silent observers of the world around us. I would stare at them, noticing that when they were wet on the beach, they looked far more fascinating than when they were dry back home. I would pick them up and look closely, admiring the subtleties that made each one unique and beautiful. Even what some would call the ugly ones had something interest-

ing about them. Some stones would develop faces as I gazed at them. I could clearly see and feel that although these looked plain and ordinary, each had a special story to reveal.

Going to beach in the morning soon became something I felt more comfortable doing. I looked forward to discovering new stone-friends as much as I enjoyed walking alone in silence. Even my baby steps became lighter, although never bouncy. My inner artist awakened in some small way and begged that I bring more than a few orphaned stone friends home with me. First, in my pockets—but there were never enough pockets. Then in a fabric tote bag, but I had concerns it would rip from the weight. One miraculous morning, I found an abandoned golf ball bucket on the beach (how lucky was that!) and that became the Perfect Bucket for collecting stone friends. Because there were so many beautiful stones that the ocean delivered to my beach, I would come home from each visit at least five pounds heavier, but somehow, feeling slightly less burdened.

I live in a tiny garage apartment with one all-purpose room that I call my cave because I like to hide there. But, it's a bright cave that faces the ocean and sunsets. At night, I would sit on my couch by my lamp and examine the stones to find their faces. With intense focus, I'd rediscover the special features that made me put them in my Perfect Bucket. I'd find those faces and use a paint pen to bring each one to life. My stones were no longer inanimate objects. They started to awaken.

It didn't feel like I was "making art." There was a silent dialogue between the stone and something inside me that was from my old life. The one before Kate died. I felt I was

helping the stone grow, as if it were a hard seed that I was able to make sprout.

It doesn't take a psychologist to see the symbolic meanings here. I was, after all, picking up things that appeared life-less—even dead—and bringing them home, giving them faces and making them come alive. I even gave a name to each individual stone and wrote their unique stories. Collectively I called them The Stone People Tribe. As a newly grieving mother, it's not surprising that my subconscious would steer me to find these slumbering egg-shaped rocks to give life to. My relationship with the beach stones gave birth to something I never saw coming.

Earlier in this book I said that when one has a life shakeup, it feels like your identity has blasted to pieces. You feel like a strong mountain that has been reduced to a pathetic pile of meaningless gravel. As I looked at these beach stones, I re-alized these too had once been mountains…maybe part of a vast mysterious continent, now submerged. Maybe a glorious and famous mountain, once upon a time. And all the rough and rhythmic movement of the ocean currents had spun these mountain pieces around so many times and smoothed their jaggedness…and shaped them…into a different version of who they were. They were given new identities: first, by the ocean that broke them and then smoothed them, and then by the part of me that remembered how to create. They became lovely oval stones that felt so good in my hand. So good that I couldn't resist taking them home with me. Yet, if they hadn't gone through all their turmoil, they would still be jagged stones lying at the bottom of the ocean, and I would not be picking them up and admiring their every angle. They had to go through the churning in order to be

reborn. And born they were, into multi-hued geological treasures that I admired far more than any faceted gemstones in a jeweler's showcase.

I continued to find faces in the stones, and The Stone People Tribe grew. Because of my tiny apartment, I decided to sell my Stone People at an upcoming metaphysical gathering I was scheduled to speak at. I'd committed to this event several months before Kate's passing and I kept my promise. With eight months of grieving experience behind me, I decided I would talk to the audience about this very subject: grief. Delivering this talk at a metaphysical conference was emotionally hard, as well as risky. People attend these events to be uplifted and inspired, and I wasn't sure my topic was apropos. As hard as it was to speak to over 400 people that day, I received a standing ovation and that talk became the basis for this book.

Everything an artist creates becomes their child. Half of my children in The Stone People Tribe were purchased by attendees at that event and now live in homes in the US and overseas. It delights me to imagine that *my kids* now have places of honor in their new homes. With each, I included a birth certificate of sorts—a written story—and a wooden pedestal to make sure that my Stone People received elevated status in their new dwelling. The joy I saw in people's faces as they discovered and purchased their new stone friend was priceless. I felt slightly more alive again.

As The Stone People Tribe grew larger in my apartment, I decided to find smaller stones to draw on. They were too tiny to draw faces on, so I drew swirls and hearts on them. I started making these stones as gift tokens for a few friends.

I drew hearts on one side and "You are Loved" in a fanciful script on the back. I watched the delightful reaction of my friends as I gave them these stone gifts. Their smiles made me smile, even if for a few minutes.

As I drew the hearts on the small stones, it occurred to me that Kate would have loved them. I could see her face lighting up if she were to receive one. It was then that I decided to make more of them and hide them in public places for strangers to find. They were left on park benches, fence posts, outside the post office, in parking lots, and on the beach where they came from. I didn't sign the stones, and initially there was no message attached, only "You are Loved" written on the back of each one. A simple message from the universe to the finder. I made each stone, imagining that Kate (or someone like her) would be the one finding that stone. In that moment when she'd find my hidden stone, Kate would feel loved by something bigger than either of us, and it would replace disheartening feelings with a belief in something magical, tangible and real.

Something magical did begin to occur. Within my heart, I started to feel more balanced. Life wasn't great—I still cried a lot—but I started experiencing pockets of contentment, and that was big. The thought of brightening someone's day with a special stone created

I UNDERSTAND

~ why children love stories
~ why teenagers lie
~ why people fall in and out of love
~ loss of any kind, sucks in all ways
~ why people call in sick
~ why artists create & nature destroys
~ why crazy people snap
~ why mysteries are better left
that way
~ that smiles can be medicine
~ that memories can be friend & foe
~ that the Tin Man was
misinformed

BUT I DON'T UNDERSTAND
what
my
LIFE
has
become.

enough joy to begin to tip the scales of grief. Tears flowed daily, but there was a creative force carrying me forward, encouraging me to leave stones in secret spots, awaiting discovery by a random stranger, a keeper of my love for Kate.

I didn't stick around to see who found the stones. I believe that each stone will find the exact someone who needs it. Although the wound in my heart was still painfully raw and tender, making stones helped with healing. People were "liking" the photos of the stones I posted on my Facebook page and seemed eager to be the one to find my "love stone." Inquiries about what type of paint I used and how to make them were coming in too. It made me happy to tell others how to make them and how easy it was. After all, everyone can find a stone and everyone can draw a heart. Like a modern day Hansel and Gretel, I was leaving a trail of pebbles that enabled me to find my way back home. Three months after making my first heart stones, on a lonely Fourth of July filled with too many memories, I created a Facebook community and named it The Abundant Love Project. The goal was to engage others to make these stones and leave them for strangers in their area. We now include notes with each stone, telling the finder who we are and to post a photo.

Acts of kindness, when ignited by a spark of creativity, can be habit forming and contagious. Within the first month over 1,100 people joined the page and started creating their own "love stones" for strangers. Hand-painted stones carrying messages of "You are Loved" have been found in the US, Europe, Israel, the UK and Australia. Please visit us or join in at www.facebook.com/AbundantLoveProject.

A group of 200 children at a day camp in New Jersey made

There's a
HOLE
in my
Heart
AND IT'S
SHAPED
like
you.

stones and posted proud photos of their creations that were left near a local senior center. Seeing those kids brought joy to my inner world. I don't know how far this project will reach but there is movement in my heart where thick scar tissue wanted to form. One lonely stone made a ripple into the world, and it's touching the lives of those who make the stones and the keepers who receive them. A young man in Australia found a stone wrote a very enthusiastic message letting me know—with F-words galore—that he loved this project and thought it was #%*! awesome. I could see Kate smiling and saying that too.

Like the waves that gently washed the stones onto the beach, and The Abundant Love Project too, creating from within grief can give life some forward movement. Feelings of being alive may wash over you even if only for minutes at a time. My aliveness came from creating something that gave to people. I felt like the drowning person who was giving out life vests to others, and then having them save me.

Like the caterpillar-turned-butterfly in this story, my perspective started to shift ever so slightly. And like the nocturnal owl, new wisdom was gained by going through the dark times and seeing what others could not. The first stages of healing were realized through a series of small steps through unknown terrain. Transformation was occurring in tandem with my grief: the trails were merging into one path leading me back to this thing called life.

Inside every some*one* is a some*thing* that sustains us throughout our days. Whether it's called an indomitable

i want you to be with me, more than i want to be with me.

spirit, an energy force, eternal spark or a soul, it acts as a scaffolding that we drape our ideas, thoughts and plans on. It provides a framework that sustains us when all else falls away. Each of us has this, and although the jolt of a Lifequake will rip that structure apart, eventually the pieces can reconnect and rebuild. It repairs like a broken bone. Learning to walk after mending a broken leg is done in baby steps. It takes time, patience, help, effort and being easy on yourself.

Getting to the point where you begin to feel slightly alive again is different for everyone, and it can come in many ways. In my story, it took the beach walks and the stones to begin to pave a path through my journey of loss and provide me with solid footing. Sometimes I still become lost, and then I retrace my steps to find that path again. Don't lose hope when there are days that provide no path or direction. Like a rainy day, those days are best spend within.

Once you get through to the other side of a Lifequake and are able to rebuild, one may look back on what they have experienced and see it through a different lens. This is a process, and personally I'm not on the other side of this yet, but I know that time is my companion and it may take years, perhaps decades. The reservoir of grief may always be present in your heart, but allowing other good experiences to enter will provide balance.

For those of you recently jolted by a Lifequake, please know that it's normal and necessary to sit with your feelings: all of them. The ones that touch your heart in a good way and the ones that make it ache. Move through all the layers of

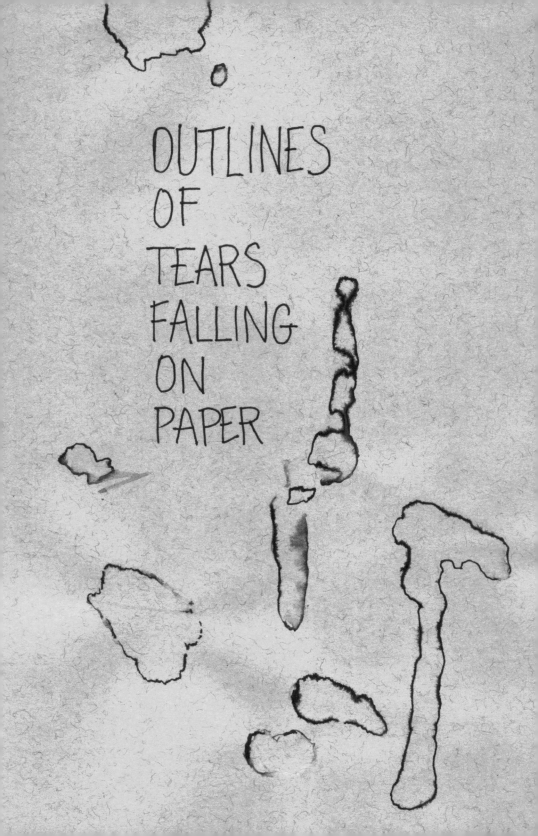

OUTLINES
OF
TEARS
FALLING
ON
PAPER

your emotions. Recognize them for what they are: they are reminders of your ability to love. Remember that self-judg-ment and guilt are immobilizing emotions that can cripple if allowed to reside permanently. Do seek help when the intensity of your loss outweighs your ability to carry it.

This can make all the difference. It did for me.

And please remember this...

PAIN
lives in
your heart
and so
does
LOVE.

GRIEF
may
dim
the light
of the
sun,
but it
cannot
extinguish it.

MY Love for you
IS LIKE A
waterfall
THAT
HAS
NO
GROUND
TO
CATCH
IT

Always
honor
what you feel,
even when
LOVE
feels like a
waterfall
that has
no ground
to catch it.

Allow feelings to move through you as you reconcile them:

write in a journal

doodle

take a walk

play with a pet

go to a garden,

go to the beach

or the mountains.

Seek professional help

see a psychic

eat cookies

throw rocks at the ocean

listen to music

or

listen to the quiet.

Do something that helps you get to the next moment. Even when the space between moments feels like a dark chasm. Take deep breaths. Release through tears. Ask friends to help by listening honestly, and thank them for hearing your pain.

Cry. Wear sunglasses to hide puffy eyes, and have tissue boxes in every room and in your car. Grief is messy.

Scream, doubt everything, and know that somewhere inside you, inside that black hole, your light is still present but it cannot escape the powerful force of this trauma. In time, you

THE ONLY WAY THROUGH IT IS TO DO IT.

will find your way your way out of the tunnel. You *will* pop through to the other side, where your life will contrast to the one you had. Life may not "get better," but it is still life and will continue, delineated by dawn and dusk.

From where I am now, I can see faint colors starting to return to my life, in very small and very subtle ways. It's not a rainbow—not even close—but the light is there in varying degrees. It's there for you too, so don't despair.

Stay true to what's inside you and flow with what you're feeling. Enliven your inner artist, knowing that you're the sculptor with the gentle hands to shape your life into something meaningful to you, and you alone.

Hang in there: life does this to all of us at some point. No one leaves this world unscathed in some way. You *will* get through it. You will rebuild in the spot you choose. Friends and family will help you, *if* you can lovingly see past the times when something they say or do upsets you. Remember, friends and family are not mind readers and won't know how to interpret your moods, changing feelings, or when you need them near and when you need your space.

Help them to navigate your new environment by giving them a compass and showing them how to read your new map. Help them avoid land mines by pointing out the fragile parts of your terrain, and also point out the resting spots where they are welcome to linger. Sharing your map with friends and family will avoid the common scenario of having them disappear from your life when you need them most. It's commonplace for some relationships with friends or family to drift away regardless. For those who stay, find ways to help

i MISS you
1,000 times
a day, and,
I THINK OF
YOU
1,000,000
times
MORE

them build a bridge from their world to yours. What may seem like friends and family forgetting you in your time of pain is actually them *not knowing how to approach you* or where to begin a sensitive conversation. Help them learn.

When you rebuild after a Lifequake, you will have a new view from the landscape you settle into, and nature will welcome you there. In time you will invite others over, and they will embrace everything about you and gently acknowledge the journey that got you there.

Release self-judgment, remembering again that there are no fault lines in a Lifequake. Keep a steady eye on how far you've come and the many small-but-difficult victories you achieved. It takes an enormous amount of stretching of your comfort zone to get through each day. You have done the hardest work that can be asked of a human. Please remember to honor your progress, be kind to yourself and cherish each moment with those you love, and those who love you.

The following pages are more excerpts from my journal. I share them to let you know your grief is real, it is acknowledged, and you are not alone or crazy in your thoughts and feelings. Depression is real and acknowledged and should be expressed. I encourage you to find ways to express yourself with your own voice, words, doodles and creative outlets.

DISBELIEF.

No matter how you
define it,
analyze it, or
dissect it,
It is the one
word that
describes
MY PRESENT
STATE,
as it applies to all
things.

We all expect that someday
our parents will pass before we do...
BUT to bury a spouse, sibling or
CHILD
is an
unimaginable
day
marked on an
unthinkable
calendar
and
filled with
inconceivable
grief
and
uncontrollable
tears.

I wish i could turn down the → VOLUME on the PAIN in my heart

SAD CRYING LOST EXCRUCIATING AGONY TAKE ME NOW

i

just

can't

do

this

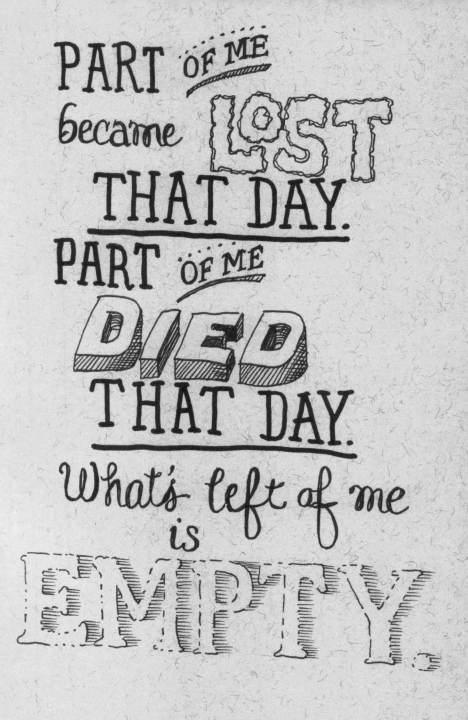

PART OF ME
became LOST
THAT DAY.
PART OF ME
DIED
THAT DAY.
What's left of me
is
EMPTY.

i
am
alone
and
lonely.

and
nobody
notices.

Death

snuck into my house
one night
and stole
that which
was
most Precious
to me.

Forever
is
too long
TO BE
without
YOU.
❀

i am "Pretend Living"

because the real me was murdered.

RIP.

EVERY
MORNING
I WAKE UP

and remember
that
YOU ARE GONE.

i try so hard
to do the 'THINGS
THAT
Alive People
DO.
BUT
i still don't feel
ALIVE.

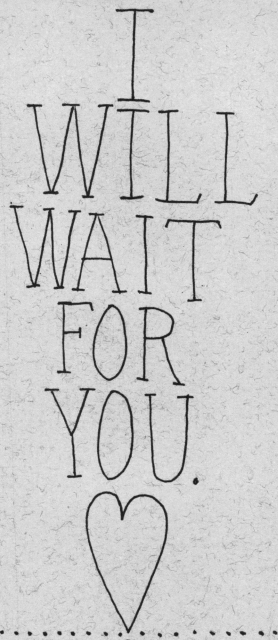

I
WILL
WAIT
FOR
YOU.

I MISS YOU

I MISS YOU

I MISS YOU

I MISS YOU

I MISS YOU

I MISS YOU

I MISS YOU

I MISS YOU

I MISS YOU

I MISS YOU

I MISS YOU

I MISS YOU

I MISS YOU

I MISS YOU

I MISS YOU

I MISS YOU

I MISS YOU

I MISS YOU

I MISS YOU

I MISS YOU

IT

NEVER

STOPS.

♡

if i
carry you
in
my heart
we will
never
be apart.

KATE
In Loving Memory

"For my ally is the Force, and a powerful ally it is.
Life creates it, makes it grow. Its energy surrounds us
and binds us. Luminous beings are we, not this crude
matter. You must feel the Force around you;
here, between you, me, the tree,
the rock, everywhere, yes."
- Yoda

Deborah DeLisi has been a creative expressionist all her life, from the moment she first held crayons and pencils to draw and write childhood poems. Throughout her life she has channeled her creative talents to bring people a sense of joy and self-discovery through her art, writing, presentations and workshops. Her creativity is a companion to her personal life challenges, and she has ridden that metaphorical dragon out to the cosmos and then back to the microcosm deep within many times. Throughout it all, Deb maintains a belief in the power of love and the importance of living. In her long and distinguished career as an artist, her greatest creations always remain her two daughters, Sara and Kate.

Deborah DeLisi Website:
  www.DeLisiArt.com

Facebook Pages:
  • DeLisi Art page: www.facebook.com/DebDeLisiArt
  • The Abundant Love Project page:
    www.facebook.com/abundantloveproject

Workshops and Speaking Engagements:
  If interested in having Deborah speak at your workshop,
  please go to www.DeLisiArt.com and click the Contact
  Page, and send a message with your specifics. Deb
  teaches a variety of workshop and currently leads a local
  group where she supports bringing balance to grieving
  parents. The meetings are a safe space to express the
  challenges of deep loss and grief, while also participat-
  ing in creative and meaningful activities. She also
  enjoys teaching groups how to draw on stones, journal,
  and make group mandalas using natural materials, and
  engage with life. Deb says she will likely cry and laugh at
  most workshops she teaches. It's the emotions that make
  us human.

Join the Community:
  Visit www.DeLisiArt.com and click the "Connect with
  Deb" button at bottom of the page

CPSIA information can be obtained
at www.ICGtesting.com
Printed in the USA
LVHW070240250920
667092LV00010B/955